Essential Science ✓

Forces & Friction

D1331074

Peter Riley

W
FRANKLIN WATTS

This edition 2010.

First published in 2006 by Franklin Watts
338 Euston Road, London NW1 3BH

Franklin Watts Australia
Hachette Children's Books
Level 17/207 Kent Street, Sydney NSW 2000

Editor: Rachel Tonkin
Designer: Proof Books
Picture researcher: Diana Morris
Artwork: Ian Thompson

Picture credits:
Leslie Garland Picture Library/Alamy: 6t, 7b; Lowell
Georgia/Corbis: 19c; Martin Harvey/Alamy: 12t;
Joe McBride/Corbis: 23t; Model Images Ltd/Alamy: 15c;
NASA: 11; Phototake Inc/Alamy: 12b; Reuters/Corbis: 14t;
Alwyn J. Roberts/FLPA Images: 20t; Richard Hamilton
Smith/Corbis: 17; Stockshot/Alamy: 10t; Topfoto: 21t. 23t;
Clive Tully/Alamy: 4; D.P.Wilson/FLPA Images: 18.

All other images: Andy Crawford

With thanks to our model Gloria Maddy

A CIP catalogue record for this book
is available from the British Library

ISBN 978 0 7496 9606 1
Dewey Classification: 531'.133

Printed in Malaysia

Franklin Watts is a division of Hachette Children's Books,
an Hachette UK company.
www.hachette.co.uk

CONTENTS

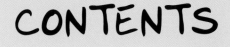

FORCES AND FRICTION

A force is a push or a pull. Close this book and then open it again. You used pushes to close it and pulls to open it. All kinds of movements are due to pushes and pulls.

This dog is pulling on the lead.

What forces can do

A force can make something: start to move, go faster or slower, change direction or stop. Forces can change the shape of things by squashing, stretching, bending or twisting them.

Many kinds of forces

You cannot see forces but you can see and feel their effects. A force that pulls on us all the time is the pull of gravity.

Gravity pulls us towards the Earth. Another force is friction which occurs when two surfaces rub together. When you ride your bicycle you can feel a force called air resistance pushing against your face. If you try and walk in a swimming pool you feel a force called water resistance slowing you down. One of the most fascinating forces is magnetism which only pulls on iron and steel.

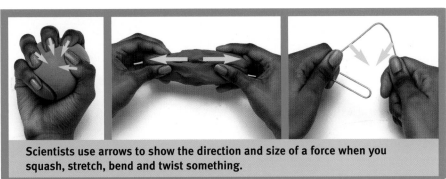

Scientists use arrows to show the direction and size of a force when you squash, stretch, bend and twist something.

Pointing the way

Even though a force cannot be seen, scientists show where it is in a picture by drawing an arrow. The arrow shows the direction in which the force is pushing or pulling. The size of the arrow shows the size of the force.

Measuring a force

A force meter is used to measure a force. It measures the strength of the force in units called newtons (N). You can judge the strength of a small force without a force meter if you remember that an average-sized apple pushes on your hand with a force of approximately two newtons.

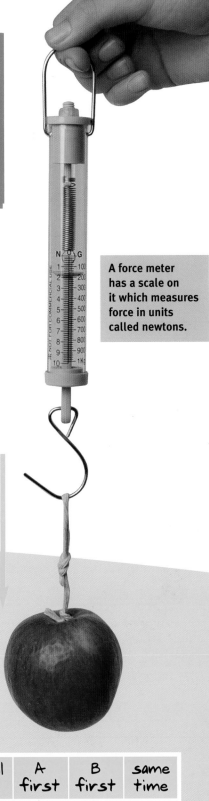

A force meter has a scale on it which measures force in units called newtons.

Use the data

When scientists do experiments, they make observations and record them. This information is called data. It may be in a table, bar chart or line graph. Collect some data about how paper falls to the ground by trying this activity. Take two pieces of paper and screw one up into a ball (A) and make a fold in the other (B). Hold the two pieces at the same height and let them fall. Record which one reached the ground first. Repeat three times and record your results in a table like this one. How does your data compare? Answers to all the questions in this book are on page 31.

Trial	A first	B first	same time
1	✓		
2	✓		
3	✓		
4	✓		

MAGNETS

Magnets have the power to pull certain kinds of metal objects to them. Some magnets are made by using electricity and are called electromagnets.

Where does the name come from?

Over two thousand years ago a rock was found that made pieces of iron cling to it. It was discovered in a country called Magnesia, which is now a part of Turkey. The rock was called magnetite after the place it was found. When metal bars were made that could attract iron, they were called magnets.

The arrow shows the magnetic force pulling on the paper clips.

Magnetite is a rock which contains iron.

Making a magnet

A small bar of iron or steel can be made into a magnet by stroking it with magnetite. Once a magnet is made, it can be used to make another magnet by stroking another bar of iron or steel with it.

Magnetic metals

A magnet does not pull all kinds of metal objects to it, just objects made from iron and steel. Other metals, such as aluminium, copper and gold, are not pulled towards a magnet.

Uses of magnets

You probably have magnets on your fridge door. The magnet pulls on the steel in the fridge door to stay in place. The magnetic force is so strong that it can even pull through paper if you hold up a message with it. There is also a magnetic strip just inside the fridge door. It holds the door shut by pulling on the steel frame around it. When you open a fridge, you pull against the magnetic force.

Magnets are used for many things, like keeping the fridge door shut.

The electromagnet pulls on the steel in the car's body.

Electromagnets

An electromagnet is made by winding wire around a piece of iron. When electricity passes through the wire, the iron turns into a magnet. When the electricity is switched off, the iron loses its magnetism. Electromagnets have more uses than ordinary magnets. Very powerful electromagnets are used in scrap yards to move cars around. Some electromagnets can be quickly switched on and off. They are used in the speakers of a radio, CD player or TV to make vibrations we hear as sound.

Strength of magnets

This bar chart shows the strength of four magnets by how many paper clips they can hold.

1 How many more paper clips could D hold compared to C?

2 How many times stronger is B than A?

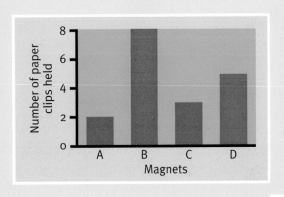

MAGNETIC POLES

The most powerful parts of a magnet are the poles. They are at each end of a magnet.

The Earth's magnet

Scientists believe that there is iron at the centre of the Earth which behaves like a huge magnet. One end of this magnet is near the Earth's North Pole and the other end is near the Earth's South Pole.

North and South Poles

If a magnet is put on a piece of wood floating in a bowl of water, something special happens. The magnet turns so that one end points towards the Earth's North Pole and the other end towards the Earth's South Pole. The end pointing towards the North Pole is called the north-seeking pole, or north pole of the magnet. The end pointing south is called the south-seeking, or south pole of the magnet.

Pushing and pulling

If the north poles, or south poles, of two magnets are brought together, they push each other away. They are said to repel each other. If a north and south pole are brought together, they pull each other close. They are said to attract each other.

north

south

The magnet on the string moves towards the other magnet.

The magnetic field

The area around a magnet where its force acts is called the magnetic field. You can see it by using a bar magnet, cling film and iron filings. Wrap the magnet in cling film and put it on a piece of card. Now sprinkle iron filings around it. The iron filings make lines, called lines of force. They are closest together near the ends of the magnet which shows that the magnetic force is most powerful nearest the poles. The lines further away from the magnet have larger distances between them. This means that the magnet's force is weaker at a distance from the magnet.

The iron filings line up to show the magnetic field around this magnet.

Using a compass

A compass has a magnetic needle which can turn freely. One end points north and the other south. Below the needle there is a card showing all directions including east and west. You use a compass to work out directions by lining up the needle with north and south on the card.

A compass is used to find directions.

Repel or attract?

1 Which pairs of magnets are attracted to each other?

2 Which pairs of magnets repel each other?

A	B
N–N	N–S

C	D
S–S	S–N

GRAVITY AND WEIGHT

**If you let go of an object,
it falls to the ground.
A force is pulling it down.
We call this force gravity.**

Where is the force of gravity?

There is a force of gravity between any two objects in the universe. The force of gravity acts from the centre of each object. Most of these forces are very tiny and do not affect either of the objects, but if one object is very large, its pull on another smaller object can actually move it. The Earth is a huge object compared to you and its gravity pulls on you all the time.

This bungee jumper was pulled down by the force of gravity acting between the centre of his body and the centre of the Earth.

Many people think that gravity just pulls you to the Earth's surface, but the force pulls objects to the centre of the Earth. This is why objects fall down holes. If it were possible, they would keep falling until they reached the Earth's centre.

Weight

If an object is put on a force meter, the pull is measured in newtons. This pulling force due to gravity is called weight.

If you stand on one leg with your arms out, your muscles generate forces to stop the pull of gravity from making you fall over.

Why weight changes

If you were to take an object to the moon and weigh it on a force meter, you would find that the object had lost weight. It would be the same size because its mass (see below) had not changed. The reason for the weight loss is due to the gravity of

People are six times lighter on the moon. This allows them to move or jump about more easily.

the moon. The moon is a smaller object than the Earth, so its gravity pulls less strongly on the objects close to it. The moon's gravity is six times weaker than the Earth's gravity so objects on the moon weigh six times less than they do on Earth.

Mars is a smaller planet than the Earth but is larger than the moon. Its gravity is three times less than that of the Earth. Objects on Mars weigh three times less than they do on Earth.

Heavier or lighter?

The mass of an object is the amount of matter in it and it is measured in kilograms (kg).

Here are the weights of three masses on Earth, Mars and the moon.

1 How much does the weight of a 1 kg mass change when it moves from the Earth to Mars?

2 How much does the weight of a 2 kg mass change when it moves from the Earth to the moon?

3 How much does the weight of the 3 kg mass change when it moves from the moon to the Earth?

4 Where would it be easiest to climb a steep hill, on Earth, Mars or the moon?

EARTH	
Mass (kg)	Weight (N)
1	10
2	20
3	30

MARS	
Mass (kg)	Weight (N)
1	3.3
2	6.6
3	9.9

MOON	
Mass (kg)	Weight (N)
1	1.6
2	3.2
3	4.8

ELASTIC MATERIALS

When an elastic material is stretched then released, it springs back to its original length due to a force called tension.

Rubber, plastic and metal

Rubber is an elastic material made from the juice of the rubber tree. Elastic plastics, which are made from chemicals in oil, look and act in a similar way to rubber. Steel is a metal which has elastic properties when it is made into springs. You can read about springs on page 14.

The tension in the elastic material in the trampoline pushes these children into the air.

Tension

When an elastic material is pulled, a force develops in it that pulls in the opposite direction. This force is a strain force called tension.

Pulling against the tension in these ropes helps to build up this athlete's muscles.

Releasing the tension

If the pull on an elastic band is slowly decreased, the elastic band goes slowly back to its original shape. However, if the pull on the elastic band is suddenly removed, the elastic band moves very quickly – or snaps – back to its original shape. You can see tension in action on a trampoline. If you jump on a trampoline, your weight pushes down on the elastic material to create tension which then pushes you back into the air. Similarly, in some toys you can stretch or twist elastic bands to create tension and make the toys move by letting go. If the tension in an elastic band cannot match the pulling force that is stretching it, the elastic band snaps.

Using the tension

The wood of some trees has elastic properties and has been used to make bows for centuries. When the tension is suddenly released in a bow it provides the force to fire an arrow into the air. The tension in elastic bands is also used for more peaceful purposes – holding a bundle of letters together.

A tension force develops when an elastic band is twisted. It can be used to spin an aeroplane propeller and make the aeroplane go forwards.

Stretching elastic

An elastic band had weights added to it. After each weight was added, the length of the elastic band was measured.

1 How much does a weight of 10 N stretch the elastic band?
2 What happens to the length of the elastic band as the weight pulling on it increases?
3 What do you think might be the length of the elastic band if a weight of 25 N was attached to it?
4 What might happen to the elastic band if a weight of 300 N was attached to it?

Weight (N)	Length (mm)
0	100
5	110
10	120
15	130
20	140

SPRINGS

Springs are made from a metal wire which has been made into a coil. There are three kinds of springs — close-coil springs, open-coil springs and spiral springs.

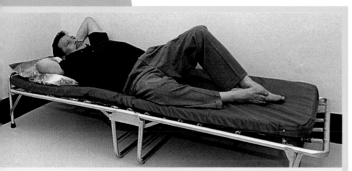

The weight of this sleeper makes the close-coil springs stretch but the tension in the springs holds him off the ground.

Close-coil spring

In a close-coil spring the coils touch each other. This means that the spring can only be stretched. When a close-coil spring is pulled, a tension force develops in the coils of metal to match it. When the pulling force is removed from the spring, the strain force makes it return to its original length.

The force meter

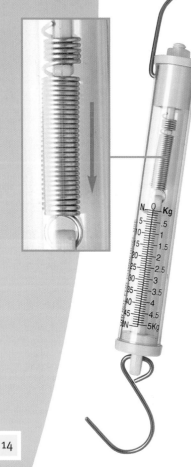

A force meter has a close-coil spring. At one end of the force meter there is a hook for attaching a weight or for connecting to objects to be pulled. A pointer on the spring moves down the scale when the spring is stretched. The strength of the force on the spring is shown by the position of the pointer when it stops moving. There are force meters with small springs for measuring small forces and large springs for measuring large forces.

Overstretching

If a close-coil spring is pulled too hard it overstretches. When this happens, changes take place in the metal which stop the tension force pulling it back to its original length. The spring then stays at its new, longer length. The metal or plastic body of a force meter stops the spring inside from overstretching.

Open-coil spring

In an open-coil spring there are gaps between the coils. The gaps allow the spring to be squashed. When the spring is pushed down or squashed, a strain force called compression develops in the coils of metal to match it. When the squashing force is removed from the spring the compression force makes it return to its original length.

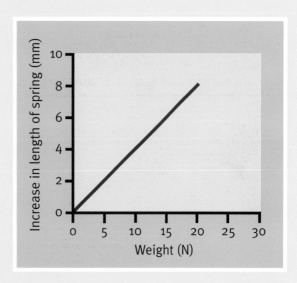

If you squash an open-coiled spring between your fingers, the force in the spring pushes back. This force is called compression.

Spiral spring

A spiral spring is made from a strip of metal that has been wound up into a spiral. As the strip is wound up a tension force develops inside. When the spring is fully wound it has a very large tension force inside it. This can then be used to unwind the spring in a clockwork device. If the spring is attached to the wheels of a toy car, the tension force can push on them and make them turn.

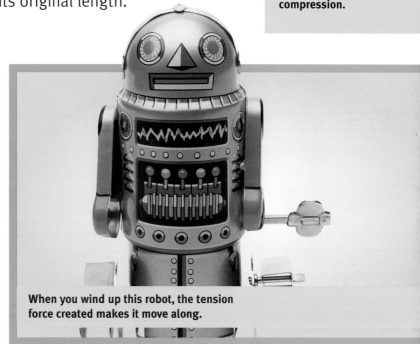

When you wind up this robot, the tension force created makes it move along.

Extending springs

A number of weights were added to a spring in turn. Each time a weight was added, the increase in length of the spring was recorded in a line graph.

1 How much did the spring extend when a weight of 5 N was attached?

2 How much would the spring extend when a weight of 20 N was attached?

3 What weight would make the spring extend to 10 mm long?

FRICTION

Friction is a force which develops when two surfaces are in contact with each other and one is pushed or pulled over the other one.

Static friction between different materials can be compared using a slope. The steeper the slope needed to make the material move, the stronger the static friction.

Two kinds of friction

There are two kinds of friction. They are called static and sliding friction. If you close this book, put it on a table and very gently push it, it will not move. Static friction is pushing against you and holding the book in place. If you push a little more strongly, the book will start to move but it will not whiz away across the table. It will move slowly because sliding friction is now pushing against you.

Measuring friction

You can measure both kinds of friction with a force meter. If you attach a force meter to a trainer and very gently pull it, the trainer will stay in place but a force will be recorded on the meter's scale. If you pull harder, the trainer will start to move and you will see the pointer move further back up the scale. This shows that sliding friction is weaker than static friction.

The grip of a trainer is being measured by a force meter.

Rough and smooth surfaces

When something moves over a rough surface a strong force of friction pushes on it. If something moves over a smooth surface a weaker force of friction pushes on it. You can easily feel this by gently rubbing your finger over the cloth in your sleeve and then over this page. You need to push a little harder to move your finger on your sleeve because of greater friction due to the surface being rougher than the surface of this page.

Increasing friction

Friction can be increased if you press two surfaces together. When you put the brakes on when riding a bicycle, the brake pads press against the rim of the wheel and friction increases so much that it soon stops the bike moving.

Reducing friction

People slip and slide on a wet floor but not on a dry one. Friction helps their shoes to grip the floor, but when the floor is wet, its surface is smoother. This means there is less friction and less grip. Oil is used in machines, such as car engines, to reduce friction between the moving parts.

People slide on ice because there is little friction to stop them moving.

Braking distance

Cars have brake pads which press against their wheels to make them stop. The table shows the distance needed to make a car stop when it is travelling at different speeds on a dry road.

Speed (km/h)	Braking distance (m)
48	23
80	53
112	96

1 How does braking distance change as a car goes faster?

2 A car decreases its speed from 112 km/h to 80 km/h. How does its braking distance change?

3 How do you think the braking distances may change if the car was driven in wet weather?

WATER RESISTANCE

It's hard work to walk through the water in a swimming pool. As you move forwards you push on the water but the water pushes back on you with a force called water resistance.

The effect of shape

If you tried to walk through water carrying a suitcase in front of you, you would find it even harder to move. The suitcase has a large flat surface. When you move it through water, the water cannot flow over it easily so it piles up in front of the suitcase and pushes even harder. This makes the water resistance very high.

When a shape with a curved surface pushes through the water, the water resistance is lower. The water flows easily over the curves and does not pile up and push with a strong force. If the shape is pointed at the front and back like some fish, the water flows over it even more easily. A shape which reduces water resistance is called a streamlined shape.

These fish have are a streamlined shape so water flows over them easily and allows them to move quickly through the water.

Testing shapes

You can test different shapes to see if they are streamlined using Plasticine. Make the Plasticine into different shapes and drop them into a tall cylinder of water. Measure the time it takes for them to reach the bottom. The most streamlined shape will fall the fastest and the least streamlined shape will fall the slowest.

The Plasticine must be dropped from the same height for each test to make the test fair.

Boats

Water resistance acts at the surface of the water, too. If a boat has a hull which is pointed at the front, water will pass under it easily and the boat will be able to move quickly. Water would push hard on a boat with a flat front and make it move slowly.

The hull of a speed boat is streamlined so there is very little water resistance to slow it down.

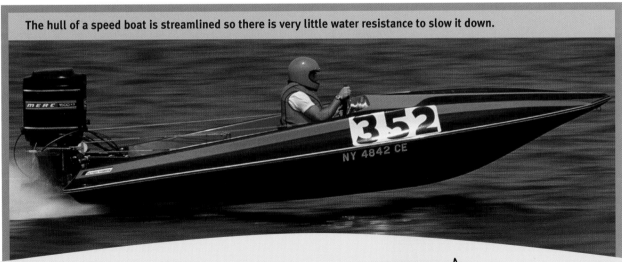

How do they fall?

The force of gravity pulls each shape down through the water and water resistance pushes up on them. Draw these shapes in order of falling (fastest first) from left to right. Draw an arrow showing the size of the water resistance on each one.

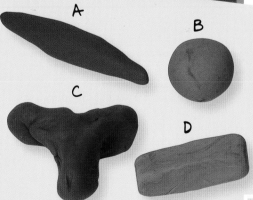

AIR RESISTANCE

Air resistance is a force which pushes on objects as they move through the air. It increases in size as the object moves faster.

Many plants produce fruits which have large surfaces to catch the wind. They rely on air resistance to push the fruits into the air and spread them out.

Feeling air resistance

As you walk along you cannot feel air resistance because it pushes with a very small force on your skin. When you get on your bike and begin to pedal, you move faster and faster and your face feels the push of the air more strongly.

Sheets of paper fall more slowly than paper balls because they have a larger surface for air resistance to push on.

The size of surfaces

If you put a closed umbrella over your shoulder and ran with it you could run quite fast. If you opened the umbrella and ran again, you would slow down. This is due to the size of the umbrella's surface moving through the air. When the umbrella is closed, there is only a small surface for the air to push on so the air resistance is small. When the umbrella is open, there is a much larger surface for the air to push on and the air resistance is high.

Wind and air resistance

You can feel air resistance when the wind blows even if you are standing still. The reason for this is due to the speed of the air. Wind moves very fast and the faster it moves the harder it pushes. If you fly a kite in the wind you can feel the air resistance pushing on the kite and you have to pull hard on the string to keep it in place.

Air resistance and cars

When you run against the wind you will find it is hard work. You will use up lots of energy pushing against the air resistance. Cars move quickly through the air so the air resistance is high. They use up lots of energy in the form of petrol. Cars are designed to be wedge shaped so that air flows over them more easily and reduces air resistance. This makes it easier for cars to move through the air and they use less petrol and make fewer exhaust gases which cause pollution.

Falling through the air

When an object falls through the air, the air pushes on it. If the object has a small surface, such as a marble, the air resistance is low and the object falls fast. If the object has a large surface, such as a parachute, air resistance is higher and it falls more slowly.

The air resistance on this parachute slows down the sky diver's fall so that he can land safely.

Which falls more quickly?

Make three squares of cloth into parachutes by tying one end of a piece of string to each corner then joining the other ends together and sticking them to a ball of Plasticine. The length of the sides of the cloth should be:

A = 6 cm; B = 4 cm; C = 8 cm.

1 Which cloth made the slowest falling parachute?

2 Which cloth made the fastest falling parachute?

3 What did you have to think about to find the answer?

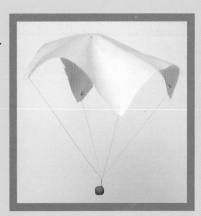

UPTHRUST

Why do some things float and some things sink?
It all depends on a force called upthrust.

Feel the upthrust

Upthrust is a force produced by water when an object is put in it. The object pushes some of the water out of the way to make space for itself. The water that has been pushed out of the way pushes back on the object with a force called upthrust. Put your hand in a sink full of water and hold it steady. You can feel the water pushing on your skin. This push is the upthrust.

Discovering upthrust

Scientists found out about upthrust in the following way. They placed an object on a force meter and measured its weight. Then they put the object in water, while still attached to the force meter and made a discovery. The object weighed less in water than it did in air!

A special can with a spout on it was filled with water and the object was put in it. The water that was pushed out of the way poured out of the spout. When they weighed the water, the scientists found that it had the same weight that the object had lost. This means that when an object is put in water, the water that is pushed away pushes back with a force that is the same as its weight. This pushing force is the upthrust.

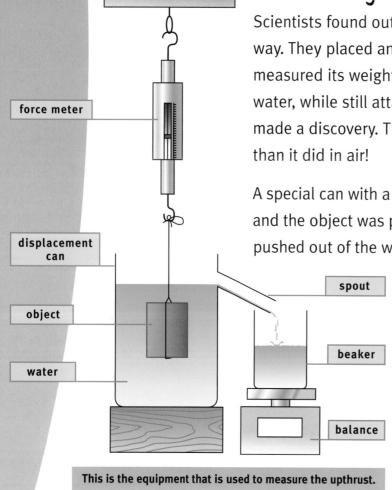

force meter

displacement can

object

water

spout

beaker

balance

This is the equipment that is used to measure the upthrust.

This wooden boat floats on the water because it weighs less than the upthrust pushing against it.

This cannon from an ancient boat sank because its weight was greater than the upthrust pushing on it.

Floating and sinking

An object will float or sink depending on its weight and the size of the upthrust pushing on it. If an object weighs less than the upthrust, it floats. If it weighs more than the upthrust, it sinks. A big, heavy boat will float as its weight is distributed over a large surface area so the upthrust is large.

Did they float or sink?

Here are the weights of five objects and the upthrust pushing on each of them.

1 Which objects floated?

2 Which objects sank?

Try doing this experiment on your own with things like a pencil or a pebble.

Object	Weight (N)	Upthrust (N)
A	10	5
B	15	20
C	12	4
D	7	10
E	8	6

BALANCED FORCES

When we study forces, we often look at the effect of one force at a time. It is important to remember that two or more forces may be pushing and pulling on an object at the same time.

Hanging around

An apple hanging from a force meter has two forces pulling on it. The tension in the force meter pulls the apple up and the apples weight due to the pull of gravity pulls it down. Fruit on trees are held in place by the same two forces but the tension is in the wood on the tree's twigs.

When a spring is squashed

If you squeeze an open-coiled spring, two pushing forces act against each other. The fingers push down on the spring and the compression force in the spring pushes it up.

The pull on a paper clip

If a paper clip is brought to one end of a magnet and released, it will hang there. The magnetic force of the magnet pulls it up and its weight due to gravity pulls it down.

Stopping a slip

If you push against a box a little and the box stays in place, two forces are acting on it. You may think your pushing force is the only one at work, but underneath the box, the force of static friction is holding it in place.

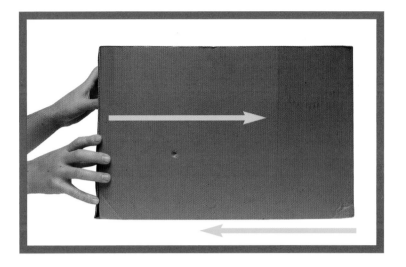

Floating

A wooden boat floating in water has two forces acting on it. Its weight due to gravity pulls it down and the upthrust of the water pushes it up.

Balanced forces

When you look at the arrows on each picture, you can see that they point in opposite directions. They are also the same size. This means that the size of one force acting in one direction is matched by the size of the force acting in the other direction. The two forces are equal so the objects do not move.

Balancing the force

1 If an apple with a weight of 2 N hangs from a twig, what is the size of the tension force in the twig?

2 If a steel object with a weight of 1 N hung from a magnet what is the strength of the magnetic force holding it in place?

3 If a model boat with a weight of 25 N floats on a pond what is the size of the upthrust?

UNBALANCED FORCES

Unbalanced forces can make a stationary object move and a moving object speed up, change direction or slow down.

A falling apple

We saw on page 24 that an apple hanging from a force meter has two forces acting on it. The forces are the same size and pull in opposite directions. If the spring in the force meter was cut, the tension force would no longer pull upwards on the apple. The pull of the apple's weight would not have a force to balance it so the apple would fall, pulled down by gravity.

The weight of the parachute is greater than the air resistance pushing up so the parachute falls.

Making a move

Boxes slide, parachutes fall and empty bottles pop up to the water surface when the forces acting on them are unbalanced.

The pushing force on the box is stronger than the friction between the box and the surface so the box moves.

Hold a bottle underwater then let go. The upthrust pushes the bottle to the surface.

Riding a bicycle

If you sit on the saddle of a bicycle and do not move, two balanced forces are acting on you and the bicycle. Your weight is pushing down and the contact force with the ground is pushing up.

When you start to pedal, three other forces begin to act on you. There is the driving force made by your muscles, which moves you and the bicycle forwards. There is air resistance, which pushes on you and the bicycle and friction, which pushes on the bicycle tyres where the tyres touch the road.

At first the air resistance is low but as you move faster and faster it rises until it matches your driving force. When this happens you move along at a steady speed in a straight line.

If you turn the handlebars, the force made by your arm muscles makes the bicycle move in a new direction.

When any object is on the move it tends to keep moving even when there is no longer a force driving it along. This means that if you stop pedalling, you will still keep moving forwards. However, the forces of air resistance and friction still push on you and because they are not balanced by a driving force you eventually stop.

You can stop even sooner if you put on the brakes (see page 17).

The bicycle moves when the forces acting on it are unbalanced.

Balanced or unbalanced forces

The table shows some forces acting on four objects.

1 Which objects are stationary?
2 Which objects are moving?

Object	Force (N)	Force (N)
A	weight 10	magnetic 10
B	weight 10	air resistance 5
C	friction 15	pushing force 15
D	weight 20	upthrust 6

CAN YOU REMEMBER THE ESSENTIALS?

Here are the essential science facts about forces and friction. They are set out in the order you can read about them in the book. Spend a couple of minutes learning each set of facts. If you can learn them all, you know all the essentials about the forces around you.

Magnets (pages 6–7)

A magnet can be made from a bar of iron or steel.
An electromagnet is made by winding wire around a piece of iron and letting a current of electricity pass through the wire.
A magnet or electromagnet pulls on objects made of iron or steel.

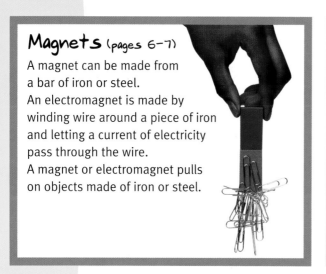

Gravity and weight (pages 10–11)

There is a force of gravity between any two objects in the universe.
The Earth's gravity pulls everything towards its centre.
The pulling force on an object, due to gravity, is called its weight.

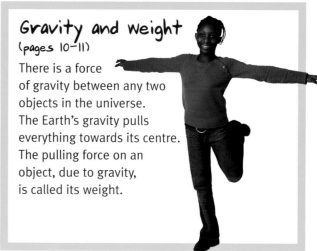

Magnetic poles (pages 8–9)

The magnetic poles are at each end of a magnet.
The two poles of a magnet are the north pole and south pole.
Opposite magnetic poles attract each other.
Similar magnetic poles repel each other.

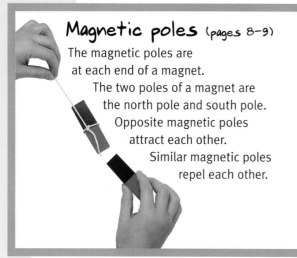

Elastic materials (pages 12–13)

Elastic materials can be stretched but can spring back to their original shape.
The force which develops in an elastic material when it is stretched is called tension.
Rubber is an elastic material.

Springs (pages 14–15)

Springs are made from a coil of wire.
Close-coil springs can be stretched to create tension.
A force meter has a close-coil spring in it.
Open-coil springs can be squashed.
The force which develops in a squashed spring is called a compression force.
A spiral spring is used in a clockwork device.

Friction (pages 16–17)

Friction develops when two surfaces rub against each other. There are two different types of friction: static friction and sliding friction.
A strong force of friction develops between rough surfaces. A weak force of friction develops between smooth surfaces.
Friction can be increased by pushing the surfaces together.
Oil and water reduce friction.

Water resistance
(pages 18–19)

Water resistance is a force which pushes on objects moving through water.
Water resistance is also a force which pushes on objects moving across the water's surface.
An object with a streamlined shape can move quickly through water or across its surface.

Air resistance (pages 20–21)

Air resistance is a force which pushes on objects as they move through the air.
As an object moves faster, the air resistance becomes stronger.
A large surface area creates more air resistance.

Upthrust (pages 22–23)

Upthrust is a force exerted by water on an object put into it.
The upthrust is the same as the weight of water displaced by an object in it. If the upthrust is greater than the object's weight, the object floats.
If the upthrust is less than the object's weight, the object sinks.

Balanced forces
(pages 24–25)

Two or more forces may be pushing or pulling on an object at the same time.
If two forces are the same size and push or pull in opposite directions, they are called balanced forces.

Unbalanced forces (pages 26–27)

Unbalanced forces make a stationary object move.

Unbalanced forces make a moving object speed up, change direction or slow down.

GLOSSARY

Air resistance The push of the air on an object as the object moves forwards.

Balance A device for weighing things.

Brake A device on a vehicle for slowing down the speed at which it travels.

Compass An instrument which uses a magnet to find directions.

Elastic A material which can spring back to its original shape after it has been stretched or squashed.

Electromagnet A device made from a length of wire coiled round a piece of iron. When electricity passes through the coil, the iron becomes a magnet.

Energy Something which allows an object or a living thing to take part in an activity, such as moving.

Exhaust gases The gases released from the exhaust pipe of a motor vehicle, such as a car.

Force meter An instrument for measuring forces. It has a scale which measure forces in newtons.

Friction A force which acts when two surfaces are in contact and one is pushed over the other. It acts in the opposite direction to the pushing force.

Gravity A force which exists between any two objects in the universe but only causes movement when one object is very much larger than the other.

Hull The part of the boat which rests in the water and supports other parts of the boat.

Iron filings Tiny pieces of iron.

Lines of force Lines which show the strength of the magnetic force in different areas around a magnet.

Magnetic field The area around a magnet in which the magnetic force acts on magnetic materials.

Magnetism The force produced by a magnetic field. The effect of a magnet on magnetic objects.

Mass The amount of matter in an object.

Metal A shiny solid, usually hard, which conducts both heat and electricity well.

Muscles Tissues in the body which allow the parts of the body to move.

Petrol A fuel made from oil which is used in car engines to provide energy for movement.

Plastic A solid material made from oil which does not conduct electricity and which can burn or melt easily.

Pollution One or a mixture of substances which are released into the environment and do not form a natural part of it. Pollution can harm living things.

Upthrust The force of a liquid pushing upwards on an object that has entered it.

Streamlined shape The shape of an object that allows air or water to flow over it easily and offers little resistance to the movement of the object.

Tension A force that is generated by an object when it is stretched.

Water resistance The push of the water on an object as the object moves forwards through it.

Weight The force of an object pressing down towards the centre of the Earth as a result of gravity.

ANSWERS

Magnets (pages 6–7)

1 2.
2 Four times.

Magnetic Poles (pages 8–9)

1 B, D.
2 A, C.

Gravity and Weight (pages 10–11)

1 It is reduced by 6.7 N.
2 It is reduced by 16.8 N.
3 It increases by 25.2 N.
4 On the moon.

Elastic Materials (pages 12–13)

1 20mm.
2 It gets longer.
3 Increases to 150 mm.
4 It might snap.

Springs (pages 14–15)

1 2 mm.
2 8 mm.
3 25 N.

Friction (pages 16–17)

1 It increases.
2 Decreases by 43 m.
3 They would be longer because water reduces friction.

Water Resistance (pages 18–19)

A, B, D, C.
A would have the smallest arrow and C the largest.

Air Resistance (pages 20–21)

1 C.
2 B.
3 The size of the cloth.

Upthrust (pages 22–23)

1 B, D.
2 A, C, E.

Balanced Forces (pages 24–25)

1 2 N.
2 1 N.
3 25 N.

Unbalanced Forces (pages 26–27)

1 A, C.
2 B, D.

INDEX